Love After Infidelity

A story of Recovering from Heartbreak, Breakup and how to Regain Relationship

BY

W. Hart

Atom Publications

*To all the lost souls who never let the darkness
of this world dim out the light inside them.*

Foreword

"Moves the heart and packs a punch... It deftly seizes hold of the heartstrings and does not let go even after it has done so. A book that is both magnificent and beautiful."

-Kirkus

"Reading this book will take you on an emotional roller coaster; you will laugh, cry, and fly through each insanely readable page. This book will make you feel all of these things."

-Halsey Jia

"A powerful book about love and the power it entails."

-Taylor Linsen

"Pleasantly surprising, warm and sweet. I found myself laughing and crying along with the characters, and in the end, I found myself falling in love with them."

-Amy Lowry

"When you finish this book, you will feel as though you have caught up with an old friend and will experience a wide spectrum of feelings. It is a novel that should not be missed by readers of any age."

-Sam Alec

A thought-provoking collection of musings about what it's like to be in love and then to have that love betrayed. This book contains a wide variety of writing styles, all of which contribute to a reading experience that is both rich and satisfying.

-Rihanna Platten

These are the kinds of stories that are most difficult in the world to tell, but this story has been done with the utmost grace. You will devour this story of honesty, suffering, and healing which is written elegantly.

-Isabella Mia

Preface

I have written this book to tell everyone who feel like they are alone, they are not. Amidst the chaos, when you have lost all of your hope, sometimes a few words can do more than you can even imagine. *It takes only one word to heal a person or to completely shatter their heart.*

Don't let negative words of others create insecurities in you. Don't let their betrayal and cold heartedness question your worth. Don't let them make you feel like you are not good enough.

You are a complete person, a person with a kind and gentle heart. You're beautiful just the way you are. Don't let anyone tell you that you're too big, too small or too dark. You don't fit into their meaning of beautiful and you don't have to. One day someone will look at you and will see beyond all your imperfections.

They will see how those small eyes sparkle when you talk about your favorite things, they will see how your belly folds when you sit on a couch, they will see how your tan skin lights up when you go out in the sunlight, they will see you trying to fit into your skinny jeans but your big fat thighs won't let you.

But you know what? They will still love you. To them you will still be pretty. Those are the people who are meant to be in your life. *So don't change for anyone because the right ones won't try to change you, they will accept you just the way you are.*

Preview

With my mind running fast and my heart racing, I took a deep breath as I stared into the mirror in front of me. Tears streaming down my cheeks, my eyes filled up with pain. I tried to take control of myself as memories played out right before my eyes.

Is this what love does to you?

Is this what forever means?

I thought love was all about holding hands, telling each other that you are the best thing that has ever happened to me. Romantic dates, candle light dinners, making each other laugh, reading books together, sharing food, and above all finding your home in their eyes.

I never knew love was about heartbreak, I never knew love was ripping other's heart and stepping on it. I never knew love was about taking the other person for granted, making them feel worthless as someone else lays in the comfort of your arms.

I thought that I would never be able to love again. I would never be able to trust another person more than myself again. I would never be able to laugh my heart out again. I would never be able to be myself again.

But little did I know that God had other plans for me.

Acknowledgements

Carly Larsson and Anna Puth never fail to provide me with sound advice at just the right moment, and for that I am quite grateful. In addition, I would want to express my gratitude to Harry Benjamin for being patient with me and for having unwavering faith in my abilities.

Stella Rogers has both grace and talent, and I owe her a debt for both. It is a privilege to have the opportunity to showcase her creative touch in these pages.

The following people — Ava Marie, Sean Oliver, Jane Noah, and Mary Patricia — have been essential to the production of this book and without them, it would not exist. I am grateful that you have invested some of your significant and precious time in both this novel and in me. I cannot express how much gratitude I feel for it.

I want to express my appreciation to Eli Norah, Miles Andrew, and Jacey Keyon for all of the motivational speeches and for their perseverance.

Last but not least, I want to give a special thanks to Justin Finn and Sophia Charlotte for the crazy stories, for making me laugh, and for showing me a different side of myself.

About the Author

W. Hart was born in the year 1963 in the country of Canada. She is the eldest of her five brothers and sisters. She spent seven years of her life in Canada before making the journey to New York City with her parents.

Her early interest in poetry and literature demonstrates that she has always had a strong connection to the English literature.

When she first moved to New York at the age of 15, she experienced feelings of instability and being lost in a foreign environment. In spite of this, she managed to successfully complete her education and started working as a teacher.

 Her first students, a group of young students who came from low-income households, were the ones who encouraged her to return to her first love: writing.

In 1986, she released her first collection of short stories. She has been a source of motivation for many others around the world. Ms. Hart uses the power of her words to encourage others to understand the strength they have within themselves and how much life has to offer by drawing on her personal experiences of homelessness, betrayal, and abuse.

TABLE OF CONTENT

ONE

Dusk

As I stepped outside in the cold breeze, I pulled my jacket closer to myself. The chilling wind sent shivers down my spine, but I did not care.

I did not care because what was happening inside me was much worse than the weather outside. With tears streaming down my cheeks, I increased my pace to reach my calming place sooner. I took a deep breath as I tried to take control of myself and my emotions. I clenched my heart as memories played in front of me.

His hands were in my hair, our fingers intertwined, our pancakes, our inside jokes.

He was my home, but now I was homeless.

It shatters you when you thought that you were finally home, you were finally loved, and you were finally in love with your soul mate. But then, someone much prettier, smarter and much stronger comes and takes over your home. Doesn't it?

I took a deep breath as I tried to get rid of my thoughts. With my hands shivering, I cleaned my stained cheeks. It has been three months, but these tears, they just don't stop; my heart still aches.

Maybe it will forever be like this. I sighed heavily as all I could see was hopelessness all around me.

"Ella, would you just wake up?" I heard my mum's voice coming from a distance.

"Ella?" She called out again

"I'm awake, mom," I answered as soon as I heard her footsteps approaching.

Stepping out of my bed drowsily, I walked towards the bathroom. As soon as I gazed at myself in the mirror, I got surprised. I was a mess. A complete mess. My hair was rumpled, mascara tracing through my cheek, my eyes all puffed up and red, and my face was swollen.

I took a deep breath as the only words that came into my mind were

"CONCEALER, A LOT OF CONCEALER"

As I got ready for college, I glanced at myself from head to toe. No more puffy eyes, no more messed up hair, no signs that this girl went through a breakdown last night.

"Perfect," I said to myself and headed for my college.

Strange stares and weird looks were all usual for me now as I sat at my lunch table alone. I started eating my bologna sandwich, which was, by the way, the only good thing in my life right now. My muscles started to tense up as soon as I saw Jennifer approaching.

Jennifer. The college's most popular and desirable girl. Men couldn't get enough of her beauty.

She took her seat right before me and spoke in a sarcastic tone.

"So, I heard Matteo cheated on you. Is this true?" She asked with curiosity and bitterness in her eyes.

"Yeah, he did," I said, controlling my tears that were just about to burst.

"Oh, I'm so sorry, honey," Her sugar-coated words continued. "I already told you he would cheat. Any guy would have cheated if he dated someone as repulsive as you. I told you to give up on him long ago, but your dumbness wouldn't allow you, and it is perfectly okay. It is now your loss."

With that being said, she stood up and left as I heard her heels clicking on the floor.

I drew a long breath and steeled myself against her words. Yet I surrendered. I ran to the bathroom because I did not want to make a fool out of myself in front of everyone.

Short breaths, shivering body, my mind messy. I tried to control myself, but I failed. Sitting on the bathroom floor, I fell to my knees and started sobbing. My pain would not go.

"Matteo," I said under my heavy breath. "Why did you do it?" I said to myself, sobbing.

After a long 15 minutes of good crying, I gathered myself up. However, I did seem a bit messy. I headed for my Math class.

Mr. Hendrickson came in just as I was getting comfortable at my desk.

As soon as we pulled out our notebooks, he began lecturing on algebra. I tried to get hold of what he was teaching, but my mind kept diverting. All I could pay attention to were Jennifer's words.

Repulsive. Dumb!

I slowly started to accept what she had told me. I started to accept that I did not fulfill Matteo's needs. Suddenly, memories began to flood back.

I remember how we laughed our hearts out as we sipped Starbucks while sitting in our car. He kept telling me jokes, and I could not control my laughter. I'll never forget him warning me to tone down my manly laughter.

He told me I dressed like every other dull girl and asked me to try something new like the other girls did. He hated my oversized hoodies and shirts.

I remember him telling me to act maturely and keep my child inside of me as he introduced me to his friends.

"Ms. Ella!" I was startled out of my little world as I heard my name.

I headed towards Mr. Hendrickson to receive my test. My eyes widened as I saw a big zero written on the top of the page. I started biting my lips out of embarrassment. Mr. Hendrickson took off his glasses and looked at me concernedly.

"Is everything alright, Ms' Ella?" he asked.

"Yes, sir," I replied with a straight face.

"You don't seem like a student who would get these grades." He continued.

"I'm sorry, sir; I will do better next time," I assured him with a fake smile.

"I believe you." He smiled back.

Given my previous academic record, I always got an A+ in every subject.

Although I was dumb in real life, I was bright in academics.

I will not let my emotions and Matteo Logan ruin the only good thing I have in my life now.

TWO

The Hazel Eyes

It was my younger sister's 11th Birthday.

Her level of excitement was beyond anything I'd ever seen before. She came into my room running to show me her white floral dress and pearl headband.

"Why haven't you still gotten ready?" She asked me, tensed up.

"I will be there on time, Selena, do not worry," I told her with an assuring smile.

"What are you wearing today?" She inquired.

I got up from bed and took out the dress from my cupboard. The straight hem of my dark green dress ended just above my ankle. A stunning string of black beads hung around its neck.

"No, No, you cannot wear this; you should wear this instead," Selena said while holding my light pink dress in her hands that ended just above my knees.

"No honey, I do not want to wear that. It makes me uncomfortable." I tried to convince her.

"But you look so pretty in this!" She continued.

"Selena, this dress makes me look so fat. I cannot make a joke of myself wearing this dress and revealing my fat thighs," I said with a straight face.

"Fat thighs? Where?" She said as she started searching in my room.

"Selena, don't be crazy." I laughed

"You are the one who is being crazy, El; I do not know what has gotten into you." She said as she left my room.

I took a deep breath and stood in front of my mirror. I examined myself from head to toe, especially my legs. They did seem fat; if I had a perfect figure and beautiful delicate legs, then why would Matteo have cheated me?

I sighed heavily as I recalled him telling me not to wear my favorite skirt with him as he did not feel good when I walked with him.

I gave up on my favorite things for you, Matt, I gave up everything I had, and I changed myself entirely to be beautiful in your eyes, and someone achieved that without even trying. Life is so unfair.

"Ella, honey, come downstairs." My mum called out.

"Coming, mother," I replied and went downstairs to see a table set with a spread of delectable treats surrounded by flickering candles and beautiful blooms. But to my bad, most of the dishes were made of potatoes and red meat or were too sugar-sweetened. I could either avoid them or have my weight increased and enjoy them. So I compromised on my happiness once again.

"Ms. Davis, I am shocked to see these results. You are one of my smartest students, but your marks are concerning me." I bit my lip once again in embarrassment as I heard Mr. Hendrickson.

"Sir, I tried my best this time." I tried to assure him.

"I hear you, Ms. Ella, but if you continue to get such marks, you will not be able to pass this course." He said with a concerned look.

"Shawn, please come here," Sir Hendrickson called out.

I turned around to see mysterious hazel eyes, a little widened, pale skin and black locks falling on his forehead.

"Yes, sir?" he asked as he stood beside me.

Woah! This dude has got one hell of a height. I thought to myself, examining how small I looked beside him. But soon, I and my thoughts were interrupted when I heard Sir Hendrickson asking Shawn to tutor me.

"What?" I blurted out.

"Calm down, Ms. Ella, it is not a big deal. Shawn is a great student and a topper in mathematics. He would help you out." He continued.

"Sir, I do not need his help; I assure you I will get good grades next time." I insisted.

"That is what you said last time." He said, putting my papers in front of me.

My ears started to turn red out of embarrassment as I realized Shawn saw that big zero on my exam paper.

"You do not need to worry, I will help, and we will surely get good grades NEXT TIME." Shawn teased as he saw my repulsive behavior.

"Yeah, sure," I said, rolling my eyes and returning to my seat.

———————————————

"So, when are you free?" Shawn asked, catching up to me as I left the classroom after my Mathematics lecture.

I halted for a moment, crossed my arms, looked him in the eye and told him, "I do not need you; just because I got bad marks in few tests does not mean I need tutoring, especially from you."

"Just because you have been excellent in academics does not mean you cannot take help from anyone." He replied, mimicking me.

"What? Are you crazy or something?" I asked, surprised at his reply.

"Nope. I am your tutor." He replied.

I took a deep breath and rolled my eyes.

"So, when are you free?" he asked again.

"Let me check." I said, looking at my watch and replied, "Never."

"Look, miss, Sir Hendrickson has assigned me this responsibility, and I take my responsibility very seriously, so you better cooperate." He replied in a simple tone.

I remained silent and replied, "After 5:00 pm on Friday."

"Okay." He said, turned around and left.

I opened the door on hearing the doorbell to see Shawn standing on the doorstep.

"Excuse me?" I blurted out, my eyes wide open.

"This is not how you welcome a guest. Do I have to tutor you on these things, too, now?" He replied in a simple tone."

"I am sorry; I just was not prepared for this," I told him.

"No problem." He said, entering the home.

I offered him a seat in the lounge and asked him to wait till I got my books. On my return, I saw Shawn having a chitchat with my mum.

I asked Shawn to come to the study room as it would be a better place to focus. We arranged the books and then opened the exercises. He started explaining to me the first question. He was halfway through the first question when I lost focus.

Thoughts started to gather in my mind that no matter how much Shawn tried, I would not be able to do it. I need to be more vital to solving these questions.

I stared at the floor as Shawn's words started disappearing in the background. Suddenly, he pinched my arm so hard that I came out of my little world of thoughts.

"What the hell is wrong with you, Shawn?" I said, my eyes starting to well up, not from the pain but from the thought that I could not even solve these simple mathematics problems.

Before he could respond, I ran upstairs, leaving Shawn and my books behind.

THREE

Calm in the Chaos

"Are you okay?" a message popped on my phone as I lay on my bed with my earphones plugged in.

It has been a few hours since I got embarrassed in front of Shawn once again. He saw me crying; he saw me weak. Hugh. He would think that I'm a complete idiot.

"Yeah," I replied.

"I am sorry I just don't know what happened." I continued.

I knew that a strong reaction would be coming. I knew men and their egos. I remember Matteo always scolding me after my every crying session.

"Nah. It's completely fine; we do sometimes feel like this. Take care of yourself." Shawn texted back.

"Oh, where is his male ego? Why is he acting like he is concerned?" I thought to myself.

I wonder why I ignored his message and continued listening to my playlist.

But, something inside me became at peace. Something inside me told me that you are not alone. Everyone feels that way.

The next day I invited Shawn again, and he came on time.

As we again started to practice mathematics, I told myself not to have any thoughts and fight them no matter what.

As soon as I saw the first question that Shawn wrote, I thought this was way too hard for me. But, at the end of the question, Shawn drew a happy face.

"What's this?" I asked, pointing to the happy face.

"Oh, this means this question is straightforward and does not require much thinking." He replied calmly.

"Oh, I see," I replied as I felt a great relief.

A smile formed on my lips as my negative thoughts flew away, and after a very long time, I thought I could solve this one, if not the difficult ones.

I asked Shawn to hand me the pencil, and he followed. I started solving the question, and to my surprise, I completed it within a minute.

"Oh great, I could not even solve this question at the speed you have." He said, a little amazed.

"Thanks," I replied, feeling a sense of accomplishment.

"Can I solve the other one?" I asked

"Yeah, sure." He replied, turning the book towards me.

I crossed my arm, bit my lip, thought for a moment and then replied.

"But promise me you won't make fun of me if I can't solve it." I insisted.

"No, no, I will never." He replied

"But you did not promise," I told him.

"So you think if I use the word 'promise,' then I would not make fun of you?" Shawn inquired.

My eyes widened at his reply.

"So, you are just going to break the promise?" I asked, shocked.

He started laughing at my response.

"Okay, okay, I won't break the promise. Don't worry; I was teasing." He replied with a grin on his face.

"I won't make fun of you if you do not get this question right, I promise." He continued smiling.

With that being heard, I started writing the question, and to my surprise, I solved it within a minute again.

"These are so easy!" I exclaimed with a big smile.

"I told you," Shawn replied, noticing my reactions.

"But this one looks difficult," I said, worried, pointing to a question.

"This is a challenging question, but not one that can stump us." He joked back and started writing the question in the notebook.

He did not even realize the impact of his words. He did not know what he had just said. He did not even know that he tore down my negative thoughts with these words.

I don't like this boy; he is different. He is something I am not. He is... I was unable to find the right words to explain what was going on in my mind.

"Out of your little world, missy." He waved his hand in front of my eyes to get me back to the real world.

I was startled as I said," I am sorry."

"No need for apologies. So, first of all, let's focus on what the question is demanding." He started explaining.

We solved the question within 10 minutes, and then he asked if he could leave.

That night, after a very long time, I did not think about my weaknesses; I thought about a few strengths of mine.

———————————

I headed towards my locker after my English lecture. I felt relaxed after my encounter with Shawn yesterday.

A little sapling of hope had been planted inside me.

I put my essentials in my locker, and as soon as I shut the locker door, he was standing beside my locker with a smirk on his face.

"You want to grab coffee after the math lecture?" He asked with a friendly smile

"No, thanks," I replied in a simple tone.

"Oh, okay." He said and headed towards the math class.

I liked that he helped me out, but I could not get close to him. Never will I allow anyone to get close to me in any way. I cannot stand another heartbreak, and I cannot stand another betrayal. I understood that no matter how sweet and caring he acted, I will get rid of this guy and anyone who tried to get close to me.

———————

The following Friday, a text appeared on my phone screen as I walked back home from college.

"Ready for today's session?"

It was Shawn. I had no energy to deal with this. I had no energy to interact with anyone, especially Shawn.

"Sorry, I'm not feeling well today." I lied

After a few minutes, my phone rang

"It's okay, take care of yourself :) "He texted back.

I rolled my eyes at his text. I went home and went straight to bed.

It was almost 15 past 5 in the evening when I woke up. I took my coat and my bag and headed for the park. I wanted to clear my mind a little, and I wanted to organize my thoughts and relax a little.

I made my way to my favorite spot in the park. I settled on the grass near the lake as I heard some birds chirping in the background. I started taking deep breaths to calm my anxiety and messed-up thoughts. I started examining the things around me.

Little flowers, lush green trees, and ripples formed in the lake as a small boy wearing a yellow sweater threw pebbles.

A smile formed on my lips as I started to observe more. Kids were playing on the swings, ladies were walking on the track, and boys were playing football nearby.

I observed their moves as they passed the ball to their teammates. I suddenly recognized a familiar face, and my smile faded.

"What is Shawn doing here?" I panicked as I tried to hide my face with my hand. But, it was no use, he soon recognized me, and I saw him walking towards me with his teasing smile AGAIN.

"Hello, there, little fella." He said as he seated himself next to me on the ground.

"Hey," I replied in a simple tone.

"So, I thought you were ill." He asked in a mischievous tone.

"Yeah, I was, but I'm feeling quite good now," I told him.

He just smiled back.

"So you play football?" I asked, pulling my legs closer to me as the wind started to brush a little more fiercely.

"Yeah, sometimes." He replied

"What games do you play?" he continued. "I don't play any games. But people surely play with me." I said in a lighter and more calming tone.

"Aw, that's okay; you are a strong soldier," He said, patting my back with a smile.

I smiled back as I felt a little lighter; I felt a little more substantial from his words.

"I don't want to tell you this, but El, you are better at math than me." He said while looking out into the park.

The sun had set, and it was starting to get cold.

"What do you mean?" I asked, a little taken aback.

"You don't fail in math because you don't know the answers; you fail in math because you don't realize how smart you are. You already have this in your head that you won't be able to answer these questions." He said, looking me straight in the eyes.

I could not blink for a moment. It felt like realization had hit me like an over speedy bus with brake failure. All this time, I had these thoughts whenever I tried to study. I still had Matteo's words engraved in my heart. They won't let me breathe and don't allow me to live my life to the fullest. They tell me that I don't deserve to be loved, I don't deserve to be happy, and I don't deserve to get anything good- even the good grades.

I started biting my lip while these thoughts gathered up in my mind.

"Don't do that; you'll hurt yourself," Shawn said, referring to my lip-biting habit.

I stopped and took a deep breath. I looked at Shawn, who was busy plucking the grass near him.

"Umm… Shawn." I called him.

"Yes?" he asked, turning his face towards me.

"Thank you." I mouthed the words as if I had no energy left in me.

He smiled back.

I got up from the ground, picked up my things, and headed home. He did not ask where I was going, did not say anything, and just stared at the lake in front of us.

We both went quiet after that discussion.

FOUR

The New Doors

I stared at the ceiling as I lay down on my bed. Shawn's words were running through my mind. It was a long time since anybody told me that I was strong; I was smart.

I don't know what was in Shawn's words that made me think deeply. Was it truthfulness? Was it sympathy? I could not predict.

I unlocked my phone, opened my WhatsApp and clicked on Shawn's profile picture. His black locks and hazel eyes made my heart skip a beat.

I threw my phone immediately and made myself understand that no matter what happens, never let anybody in and never let anybody get too close.

I closed my eyes and soon had an encounter with my sleep.

———————

The next day, as I was sitting in my math lectures, I felt a pair of eyes fixed on me. I tried to see around the corner of my eyes to meet Shawn's eyes.

I looked away as soon as those brown eyes met my dark black ones.

"Why on Earth is he staring at me? Such an idiot." I thought to myself.

"I don't know what has gotten into that man. He is acting so strange." My thoughts continued.

Soon, the lecture was over, and I started walking toward the cafeteria. Shawn came and sat beside me as I sat on my usual seat alone.

"Want to grab a coffee now?" he asked with a smile.

"No. Thanks." I replied, standing up and picking up my things.

"Where are you going?" he asked.

"Somewhere alone," I replied with a gentle smile.

"Oh, okay." He replied, standing up and heading outside the cafeteria.

As soon as he left, I sat back in my seat and started eating my favorite bologna sandwich. Although I know that this might make me gain a little extra weight, I can do anything for bologna.

As I started walking home after college, it started to pour down.

"Oh gosh!" I sighed heavily.

I continued walking, hoping to reach it before these little raindrops got bigger. To my bad, it started to rain heavily soon. I took out my notebook and tried to cover my head with it but failed. Suddenly, I heard a car squeaked just behind me.

"El?" Shawn called out.

I turned around to face Shawn, pointing towards his car.

"No, thank you. And don't you dare call me El next time; it's Ella." I replied, denying his offer.

He shook his head and came closer to me.

"Will you stop being stubborn and just come?" Shawn asked

"Umm... No," I replied

"What is wrong with you, Ella?" He asked, surprised.

"What is wrong with you? Why do you always act as if you care about me?" I came back at him.

He paused for a moment and then replied.

"I do not care about you; if you get sick, then we won't be able to study and then Mr. Hendrickson will come at me." He replied in a simple tone.

Suddenly, the black clouds completely covered the whole area, and it started to rain heavier.

A flash of lightning struck, and I grabbed Shawn's shoulder tightly, scared of the lightning and the thunder.

"It is okay; everything is fine." He told me, smiling down at me.

Ugh. This height difference makes me feel so small.

At last, I gave in and seated myself in his car. I tried to maintain as much distance as I could in his two seater but I failed. Every time lightning struck, I would grab his shirt tightly and would try to seek protection from him. I could feel him smiling every time I did this.

As soon as we reached home, we both ran inside to avoid the weather. We immediately turned on the fireplace and sat beside it. My mother brought both of us towels and some more essentials. I got up to change my clothes while Shawn kept sitting there.

As I came downstairs after changing my clothes, I saw my mum setting a plate of cookies and biscuits in front of Shawn. She signaled me to come and have them too.

I sat beside Shawn and mouthed a "Thank you."

"No problem, you could always count on me." He replied, smiling.

My mother entered the room holding two mugs of hot coffee. She handed the first mug to Shawn, and as she handed me the second mug, it slipped out of her hand and…

"If Shawn had not caught the mug in time, it would have burnt you a lot, dear." My mum said, cleaning the dishes.

"Hmmm... I know." I replied, deep in my thoughts.

Shawn had left an hour ago, and after that mug slipped out of my mother's hand, he caught it just right in time. His hand had burnt a little, but still, he seemed relieved to know that I was saved.

"I'm going to sleep," I said to my mum and headed for my room, not even waiting for her reply.

I lay down and closed my eyes, but the memory of today's incident replayed.

I took a deep breath, stood up and went outside on the balcony. A smile formed around me as I remembered him telling me everything was fine as I held his shoulder tightly. I have not been told that in my life lately. I have not felt this protected in life ever.

How could he be relieved knowing that I am safe but getting his hand burnt in return?

I smiled as I knew that after a long time, I would be allowing someone in and allowing myself to trust someone.

FIVE

All We Have is Now

After my English lecture, I texted Shawn, "Where are you?"

"At the basketball." He texted back with a surprised emoji. I shook my head with a smile in his response.

I headed towards the basketball court to see Shawn tying his shoelaces. A grin formed on his face on seeing me.

"Hey," I exclaimed, a little shy.

"Hi." He replied, a little surprised.

"I just wanted to ask if you want to grab a coffee," I asked with a gentle smile.

"Wow, sure." He replied, even more surprised.

He picked up his bag, and we headed toward the coffee shop near our college. He opened the door of the coffee shop for me, and my heart melted a little. I had never been treated like this. I had only let one man inside my life, Matteo Logan. Matteo never treated me with such gestures, and so I was not habitual of these.

"Thank you," I said, passing a gentle smile. We chose to sit near the window. As we both settled down, Shawn asked me.

"How did you change your mind?"

"About what?" I replied.

"About having coffee with Shawn Howards." He said in a lighter tone.

"I just laughed a little and smiled back. Soon, the menu came, and we started looking through the options. I ordered an espresso while Shawn ordered a cappuccino.

After our order was taken, Shawn turned to me and said, "Whoever drinks the coffee first will pay the bill."

"Excuse me?" I replied, a little taken aback.

"Yup, that's the rule." He said, shrugging his shoulders.

"I won't do that; people will think we're crazy," I said, relaxing back in my seat.

"Who cares about the people? They won't even remember us once they leave this coffee house." He replied.

"Shawn, have you ever thought about getting an appointment with a therapist? If not, then kindly do." I said, laughing.

"It's your choice if you want to pay the bill; it's completely fine with me." He joked back. "Yeah, it is completely fine with me, I feel satisfied this way, and I don't allow anyone to pay the bill," I said in a lighter tone as I checked through my bag, and soon I realized my wallet was not there.

I saw Shawn holding it up in the air with a glimpse of mischievousness in his eyes.

"Just give me my wallet back," I said, trying to seize it out of his hands.

"Nope, sorry, miss, whoever drinks the coffee first will pay the bill." He replied. I gave up and sat back in my seat with my arms crossed.

Soon our deliciously aromatic coffee came, and I could not think of allowing Shawn to pay my bill, so I gave in. "fine, whoever drinks the coffee first will pay the bill." I said, rolling my eyes and laughing.

"Okay, so... 1, 2, 3 go." As soon as Shawn said this, I gulped down my coffee within a few seconds, put down the cup and looked around to see no one noticing. No one stared. No one even cared.

I then realized that I had missed so much fun in life only thinking about what people will think of me.

I started laughing as I saw Shawn's surprised face. "Did you just gulp it down in a few seconds?" he asked with his mouth open.

"Yeah," I replied, laughing.

"No words; I'm just speechless." He laughed back.

Shawn paid the bill, and we left the coffee house.

On our way back to our classes, I asked Shawn.

"Shawn, can I ask you something?"

"Yeah, sure." He replied.

"Why didn't the people at the coffee house judge us? Or, you know, staring at us." I asked, looking down at my feet, hoping he would not call me dumb for asking that question.

"That is because everybody is busy in their own life, El. Even if they would stare at you or judge you for a little while, they would soon forget it once they get out of that place." Shawn said with comfort in his tone.

"Hmm, I understand," I replied, thinking about his words.

We kept walking together until we reached our classrooms and then said goodbye.

The following Friday, Shawn arrived at my place on time, and we started preparing for our next week's mathematics exam. We spent almost 2 hours practicing, and to my surprise, I got all the questions right.

After studying for hours, we both got exhausted and decided to relax. We sat near the fireplace and started talking our hearts out.

I don't know. When I'm with Shawn, the little child inside me feels protected, and it feels that I won't be judged no matter what I say or what I do.

Soon it was time for Shawn to leave; somewhere inside my heart, I wanted to stop him, but I could not. I went to the door to bid him farewell. As he was about to leave, he turned around and asked.

"Are you coming to the prom tomorrow?"

"Umm... I don't think so." I shook my head with my arms crossed.

He looked down and paused for a moment. He took a deep breath as he looked me straight in the eyes and asked," Miss El, will you come to prom with me tomorrow?"

My heart just did a backflip, and I blushed. A lot.

"Yes," I replied, nodding as I tried to hide my blush under my big smile.

He smiled back and turned around to head for his home.

As soon as he left, I ran upstairs excited. I took out all the dresses in my closet and looked through them to find the perfect dress for tomorrow night.

I opted for my long, black silk gown that reached just over my ankles and was embellished with tiny black beads. I put that dress on myself in front of the mirror and imagined Shawn beside me.

My heart started beating faster at that thought as I smiled to myself in the mirror.

"Control your emotions, El. He is just a good friend." I confronted myself, put back all the dresses and went to bed with happy thoughts after a long time.

SIX

Stars on a Cloudy Night

I woke up at noon the next day. I haven't slept this good in a long time. I checked my phone to see a notification from Shawn and opened it to see the text.

"Good Morning. I will pick you up at 8."

I smiled and texted back. "Good Morning, sure."

I completed all my tasks before six and started preparing for the prom. I decided to curl my hair at the ends and not put on too much makeup.

It took me almost 2 hours to get ready. I was staring at my heels when I heard the doorbell ring. I immediately put them on and headed downstairs to see Shawn in front of me.

His hair was styled to perfection, and he was dressed to the nines in a sleek black tux and bow tie.

My heart melted as soon as my eyes rested on him, but I hid my emotions under sarcasm.

"It was a prom, not your wedding." I joked.

"I may not look perfect, but you, Miss El." He paused for a moment and then continued staring into my deep black eyes.

"You are just looking breathtaking."

The intensity of his gaze and his remark sent shivers down my spine. I blushed and smiled back in response.

Soon, we left my place for prom in Shawn's car. When we reached the prom, it was almost 9. We both got out of the car and headed towards the prom hall. As we were about to enter, he held my hand.

"What are you doing?" I asked, a little taken aback.

"Calm down; there were boys who had their eyes fixed on you." He responded solemnly.

I just blushed, looking at our intertwined hands.

The contrast between the chilly night and the bright, spherical, yellow fairy lights created such a magical scene that would last throughout the night. Coral pink flowers and white roses filled the space.

Couples danced joyfully in the middle of the hall while bright green lasers and flickering circular white lights whirled about them. With arms outstretched, fingers splayed, and heads held high, they danced in perfect symmetry to the trendiest tracks.

We sat on the seats around the counter and ordered a few drinks. We started grooving to the songs together and laughed our hearts out. After a few moments, Shawn held his hand out to me, and I held it as we headed to the dance floor.

The room echoed with Perfect by Ed Sheeran as we danced in symmetry. Shawn put his hands on my waist and pulled me closer as I placed one of my hands on his shoulder and my other hand on his muscular chest. I could feel his heart beating faster as we slowly started dancing to the song. I felt not only butterflies but the whole fairyland running inside me in the proximity between us.

"El?" he called my name in a low husky voice.

I looked up to get my black eyes lost in his deep hazel ones.

He stared right into my eyes and, after a few moments, said,

"I have fallen deeply in love with you, Ella Davis." I felt his heart beating faster than ever.

My eyes widened at his words; it seemed my heart had just stopped. I looked at him stunt in my place, my body shivering. I tried to reply, but soon memories flashed in front of me.

Matteo. Our laughter. Our bond. Our jokes. Our Fights. Our makeups. But above all, another woman in his arms.

My heart clenched as tears started to form in my eyes. My heart clenched at seeing Shawn having another woman in his arms. I was tired of the pain. I was tired of losing myself again. I could not bear all this again.

I let go of him, turned around and headed out. I did not dare to look back. I did not dare to see the look on Shawn's face. *I did not dare to LOVE AGAIN.*

I locked my room's door as soon as I reached home. I started taking off my jewelry and unpinned my hair. I tried to keep calm and not let my thoughts get to me, but I failed.

What an idiot he is." I thought to myself. "How could he even imagine doing this?" I took off my heels and lay down on my bed, staring at the ceiling. A tear rolled down my eye and dropped on my bedsheet. I sighed heavily as I tried to understand that I had done the right thing. But, deep down, I knew I would regret my decision later.

"I can't; I just can't." I thought to myself as more tears started rolling down my eyes. "I'm so scared to fall in love again. I'm so scared to get this close to someone else again. I'm..." I thought to myself.

My thoughts were interrupted by my phone ringing. It was Shawn. I closed my eyes as I declined the call. He started calling again, and I still declined with the heaviest heart. After a few seconds, a message popped up on my screen.

"Are you okay?" he texted.

"Yes." I texted back.

"Can I come over?" he asked.

"Just stay away from me, Shawn." I texted back.

"El, please." He insisted, and so I blocked him.

I closed my eyes and soon was asleep.

Little did I know that I succeeded in blocking him from my phone but failed to block him from my heart?

SEVEN

Fight for Your Fairytale

The following day, I woke up a little dizzy. I had a very severe headache, so I called my mum. I have received no response from Shawn since I blocked him. My mum brought me a painkiller and put me to bed again.

When I woke up again, it was almost past 2 pm. I was much better, so I decided to go out for some fresh air. I got up from my bed, got ready and headed for the park.

I tried to fight my thoughts as much as I could. Once I got to the park, I found a comfortable spot to sit and take in my surroundings. I looked around to see beautiful pink petunias planted in rows all around the park, children playing at the swings, and a group of little kids playing football. Instantly the memory of Shawn walking in his football kit with a teasing smile flashed before my eyes. His mesmerizing eyes. His strong muscles. His plump lips. His tiniest details got engraved in my heart. I started missing him. I started missing him, making me smile..... I started missing him, telling me I could conquer anything that came my way.

I jerked my thoughts to come back to reality, the present.

"He is not here, El. He is gone." I tried convincing myself as I took a deep breath.

"No matter what, El, you cannot trust him. It's not even been five months since you met him. You knew Matt for over five years, and see what he did." I made myself understand. But deep down in my heart, I knew that with Shawn, things were different. Things were not perfect, but they were just beautiful. They were the way they were supposed to be. I was the way I was supposed to be.

I got up from the ground and started walking towards home, unaware that sometimes home is not a place but a person.

I got ready, had breakfast in a hurry and headed for college. At lunch, I sat at my usual place with no one around. I started eating my spaghettis when I heard the standard clicking of the heels. I instantly recognized who they belonged to. I rolled my eyes and looked up to see Jennifer standing before me.

I ignored her, but she sat on the seat in front of me and started talking rubbish.

"I have heard that Shawn proposed to you." She said, her eyes wide.

"No, there is nothing like that," I replied immediately.

"Oh shut up, you little liar." She continued.

"I know girls like you who hide their evil faces behind an innocent one. But let me tell you, Ella Davis, you will no longer have him. He will soon get bored of your ugly face and will dump you." She mocked.

I already had enough of her. I was not someone with an ugly face; I was not someone dumb; I was not someone who would always get cheated. I was someone worthy of love and respect, and I was not going to make any compromise on that. As soon as I was going to spill all of my spaghetti over her head, I heard a familiar voice.

"Just leave her alone, or else you will regret it." I heard Shawn's voice behind Jennifer. She turned around to face Shawn.

"Or else what will you do, lover boy?" Jennifer asked in a sarcastic tone.

Shawn glared at her with a solemn expression. She went pretty afterward, knowing that if she said a word, she would regret it. She left the cafeteria, leaving both of us alone.

As I was going to call out to Shawn, he turned around and left without saying anything. He did not look at me; he did not pass his usual gleaming smile that once lit up my whole world. He just walked away in silence.

At that moment, I realized that sometimes silence is the most powerful scream.

I stared at the stars above and sat on my rooftop with my legs hanging down.

"Why didn't he look at me?" this thought had not left my mind since my interaction with Shawn two days ago. In the past few days, he had just completely ignored me. Whenever we crossed paths, he would walk away or turn back.

I missed his eyes on me. I missed his gaze. I missed the love he had for me. I missed everything that was related to him. I tried to shrug my thoughts away, afraid that maybe I had fallen in love with Shawn Howard.

Amidst my thoughts, a message popped on my screen, and I opened it to have my heart sink. It was a picture. A picture of Shawn with a girl kissing his cheek. My heart sunk in the shallow sea of dreams I had built. A few seconds later, another message came "I told you he would soon cheat on you." It was Jennifer. She was right. She was right that I would have the same fate as Shawn.

My heart started beating faster; my blood started to boil. This is not how things go. This is not how he could treat me. This is not as easy as he thinks. He will not get away with this.

I got off the rooftop, picked up my bag and barged out of the home. I started heading toward Shawn's house racing in my heated thoughts. *I cannot spare him. I will not allow anyone to take advantage of me.*

As soon as I reached his house, I rang the bell, and after a few moments, he was there with a surprised expression on his face.

"Do not dare give me that look, Shawn Howard," I snarled.

He put his hands up in the air and kept quiet.

"Do you think I am a joke?" I asked with tears starting to form in my eyes.

"What are you talking about, El? I could never think that." He replied in a soft and convincing tone.

"Then, why did you treat me like one?" I demanded.

"El, please calm down. Let's sit and talk. It is completely over my head." He replied in a gentle tone.

I stared directly into his eyes, unlocked my phone, and put up the picture in front of him.

"Is there anything more to explain?" I asked with teary eyes.

His expression suddenly changed as soon as he saw the picture.

"El?" he said, putting his hands on his mouth, trying to control his laughter. I glared at him with a surprised face.

"El, that is my sister." He continued trying his best not to laugh.

I took a deep breath as if I was finally able to breathe. But soon, my ears turned red out of embarrassment. I mouthed the words, "I'm sorry." And started looking at the floor.

Shawn just smiled back with his eyes fixed on me. Once Again!

It was so apparent that I was jealous. A lot!

It was so evident that I could not bear any girl getting close to Shawn.

It was so evident that I had once again fallen in love, but this time with my soulmate.

I did not say anything further, just turned around and started walking toward my home. I could still feel Shawn's gaze on me behind my back.

———————————

EIGHT

Live Your Life Before It is Over

As I sat beside the window of my room and stared outside, I felt a hand on my lap. I turned around to see my mom smiling gently at me.

"What is wrong, my dear?" She asked while sitting next to me. It had been two days since my last interaction with Shawn. It had been two days since I knew I had again stepped into the battleground of love.

"Nothing, mother," I replied, putting my head on her shoulder as a tear rolled off from the corner of my eyes.
"He won't hurt you, Elle. He won't betray you. There is nothing to be afraid of." She said in a soft tone.

I looked up at her, a little surprised at how she knew.

"I'm your mother, and mother knows best." She replied, smiling back as if she had read my mind.

"I don't know, mother, the fears and monsters within me won't allow me. Matt has destroyed my whole outlook on love and relationships. It feels like there is no such thing as love." I replied, taking a great sigh.

"I swore I wouldn't get my heart broken again, but then I met Shawn, and falling in love was like flying." I continued.

"I don't know, mother; he makes me feel I am strong; he makes me feel like I deserve to be loved and respected. He won't let anyone disrespect me or hurt me, even if it's me myself." I continued

"I love him, mom, and my heart knows that he is someone I am meant to be with; he is someone who completes me and makes me the best version of myself. I know he loves me despite knowing I have flaws and am not perfect." I continued speaking my heart out, not realizing how much I had fallen for him.

"El, dear, each of us has experienced that. The pain of heartbreak can affect anyone. We've all been there; someone hurts us, or we hurt them, and we want to curl up in a ball and cry. We don't realize that if genuine love and care are provided, the heart may mend. And you soon muster up the strength to fall in love once more." She said in a soft and comforting tone.

"Sometimes, the worst things that can happen to us often lead us straight to the best thing ever. To put up a battle for love is worthwhile. And it will slip through your fingers if you don't struggle." She said in a deep tone.

"I feel like I have lost all of my courage to fight, mom, but when I look into Shawn's eyes, I know I can conquer all, just for him," I replied as a smile formed on my tear-stained cheeks.

"Then, tell him and remember that nothing is stronger than two people really in love." My mum replied as she walked out of my room.

_____

"Meet me at my favorite spot at five, and don't forget to bring me flowers." I texted Shawn with a heart emoji.

"Are you serious?" he texted back.
"Let's see." I texted back with mischievousness running in my eyes.

I started to get ready to meet Shawn. I reached for my floral pink knee-length, and gorgeous sequins adorned dress. It was my favorite dress, but the insecurities I had developed over the past few years did not allow me to wear it. I curled the tips of my hair to have loose curl at the ends. I also decided to put on some light makeup.

Checking myself in the mirror, I rehearsed my proposal repeatedly in my head. I could not imagine being strong enough to give love another chance, to believe in love once again. I smiled as I imagined Shawn standing beside me and holding my hand.

I picked up my bag and walked towards the coffee house near our home. I told Shawn I had loved this place since childhood but didn't come here often.

On my way, I could only think about how things would be if Shawn said yes. I trusted him. More than myself. As soon as I reached the coffee house, I looked around to see no one. I started waiting impatiently for Shawn to arrive. Suddenly, I looked up to see Shawn, all dressed up on the other side of the road. He started walking towards me with a grin on his face and red roses in his hands. My heart started beating faster; I could feel all the butterflies in my stomach going crazy. The biggest smile formed on my face as I realized how much I loved that boy.

Little did I know that this biggest smile would soon be replaced with the most painful scream?

As Shawn was about to reach me, I heard a car honking in the background and some screams. I shut my eyes closed as I realized that forever is also a temporary thing.
A tear fell from my eye as I saw people gathering around Shawn, covered in his own blood, to get him to the hospital. Darkness surrounded me as I fell to the floor, unconscious.

"Selena, wait for me," I exclaimed, laughing. I went after Selena, who had run towards the ice cream truck.

It had been three months since Shawn passed away. It had been three months that I had not seen his face, but I still felt his presence. I know he is with me in every breath I take, in the gentle autumn wind that blows, in the rainbow after the rain and in the sun on a cloudy day.

I know he is there with me, permanently engraved in my heart. He is there with me in the lessons he taught me, in my laugh, my tears, in my strength and courage. Sometimes, you have to accept that forever means living with their memories.

I took the money out of my pocket as the man in the ice cream truck handed me two ice creams. I smiled, knowing I could eat both of them without fearing being fat and judged.
I took a bite from my favorite ice cream as my heart felt at peace.

I knew that Shawn would smile from above, seeing me like this. My heart felt at peace knowing that someone truly loves me and appreciates who I am. My heart felt at peace knowing that sometimes when someone we care about dies, we have to figure out how to carry on, not in spite of, but because of the love they leave behind.